ANCIENT

EGYPT

BY SETH LYNCH

Enslow PUBLISHING

Please visit our website, www.enslow.com. For a free color catalog of all our high-quality books, call toll free 1-800-398-2504 or fax 1-877-980-4454.

Library of Congress Cataloging-in-Publication Data
Names: Lynch, Seth, author.
Title: Ancient Egypt / Seth Lynch.
Description: Buffalo, New York : Enslow Publishing, [2025] | Series: Ancient civilizations in review | Includes bibliographical references and index.
Identifiers: LCCN 2024023822 | ISBN 9781978542709 (library binding) | ISBN 9781978542693 (paperback) | ISBN 9781978542716 (ebook)
Subjects: LCSH: Egypt–Civilization–To 332 B.C.–Juvenile literature.
Classification: LCC DT61 .L96 2025 | DDC 932/.01–dc23/eng/20240601
LC record available at https://lccn.loc.gov/2024023822

Published in 2025 by
Enslow Publishing
2544 Clinton Street
Buffalo, NY 14224

Portions of this work were originally authored by Daniel R. Faust and published as *Ancient Egypt*. All new material this edition authored by Seth Lynch.

Designer: Leslie Taylor
Editor: Kristen Nelson

Photo credits: Cover (pyramids) AlexAnton/Shutterstock, (king tut mask) Petr Bonek/Shutterstock.com, (back cover artifact) Dario Lo Presti/Shutterstock.com; Cover and series art (vintage map) Andrey_Kuzmin/Shutterstock.com, (vintage map frame) Vector Tradition/Shutterstock.com (brush strokes) ozzichka/Shutterstock.com, (font) MagicPics/Shutterstock.com; p. 5 Peter Hermes Furian/Shutterstock.com; p. 6 Glowonconcept/Shutterstock.com; p. 7 Gelia/Shutterstock.com; p. 9 AlexAnton/Shutterstock.com; p. 11 (top) anonymous Cairo Egyptian Museum/File:Narmer Palette.jpg_commons.wikimedia.org, (lower) Jeff Dahl/File:Horus standing.svg_commons.wikimedia.org; p. 12 nelo2309/Shutterstock.com; p. 13 Ihor Bondarenko/Shutterstock.com; p. 15 mi9niltu9doiroa/Shutterstock.com; p. 17 Stig Alenas/Shutterstock.com; p. 19 World History Archive/alamy.com; p. 21 Rogers Fund, 1929/Metropolitan Museum of Art, metmuseum.org; p. 23 (top) Jaroslav Moravcik/Shutterstock.com, (bottom) *The New York Times*/File:Tuts Tomb Opened.JPG_commons.wikimedia.org; p. 25 Rumlu/File:Darius I.jpg_commons.wikimedia.org; p. 27 Raymond Albert/Shutterstock.com; p. 29 Everett Collection/Shutterstock.com; p. 30 muratart/Shutterstock.com.

Printed in the United States of America

CPSIA compliance information: Batch #CWENS25: For further information, contact Enslow Publishing at 1-800-398-2504.

CONTENTS

Words in the glossary appear in **bold** the first time they are used in the text.

People of the Nile

The ancient Egyptian **civilization** began thousands of years ago! It grew up around the Nile River, the longest river on Earth. The Nile has long supplied people with water and a way to move people and goods.

LEARN MORE

The word "ancient" means very old or having been around a long time.

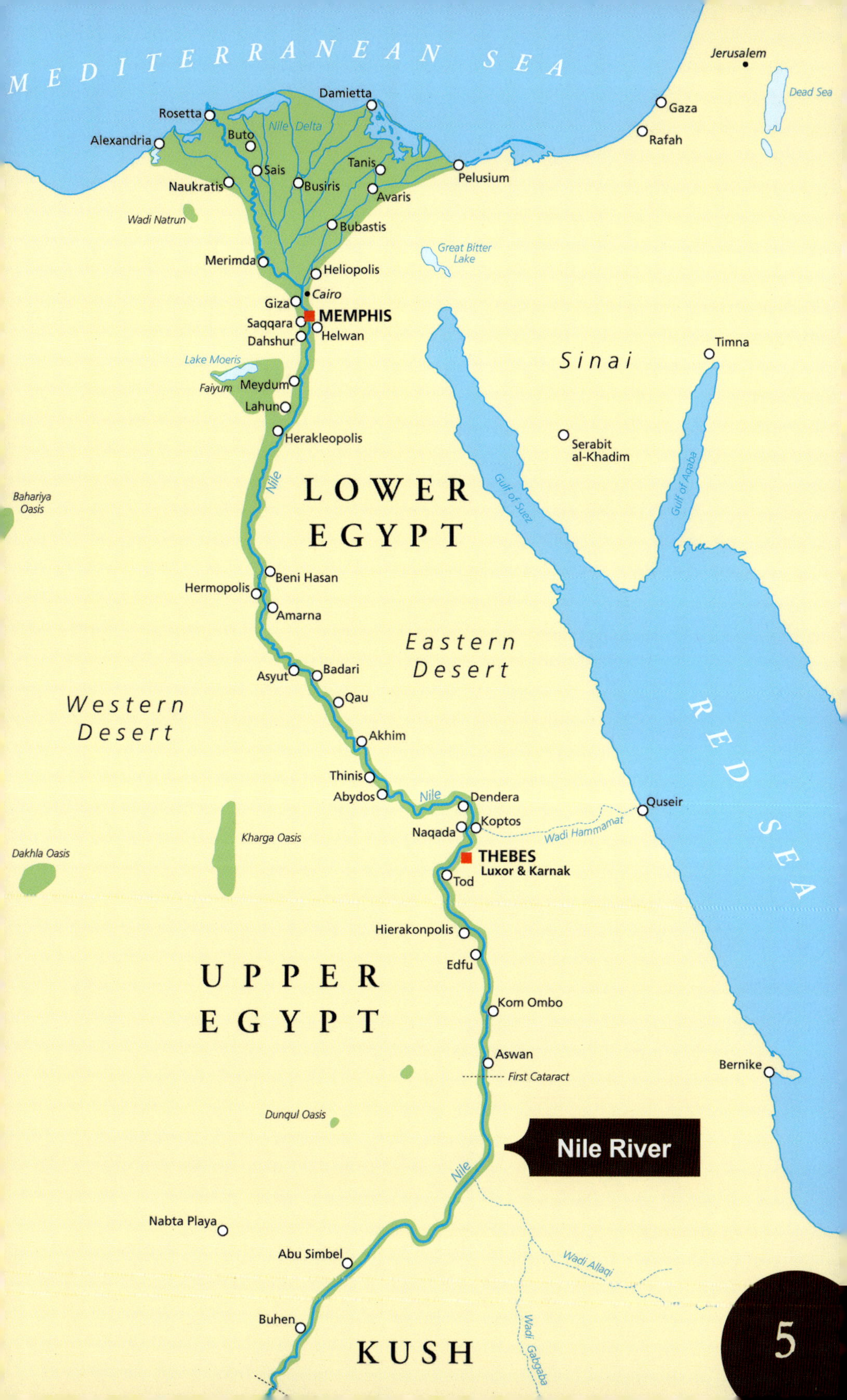

MEDITERRANEAN SEA
Jerusalem
Dead Sea
Gaza
Rafah
Damietta
Rosetta
Nile Delta
Buto
Alexandria
Sais
Tanis
Pelusium
Naukratis
Busiris
Avaris
Wadi Natrun
Bubastis
Great Bitter Lake
Merimda
Heliopolis
Cairo
Giza
MEMPHIS
Saqqara
Helwan
Dahshur
Timna
Sinai
Lake Moeris
Faiyum
Meydum
Lahun
Herakleopolis
Serabit al-Khadim
Nile
LOWER EGYPT
Gulf of Suez
Gulf of Aqaba
Bahariya Oasis
Beni Hasan
Hermopolis
Amarna
Eastern Desert
Asyut
Badari
Qau
Western Desert
Akhim
RED SEA
Thinis
Abydos
Nile
Dendera
Quseir
Koptos
Naqada
Wadi Hammamat
Kharga Oasis
Dakhla Oasis
THEBES
Luxor & Karnak
Tod
Hierakonpolis
Edfu
UPPER EGYPT
Kom Ombo
Aswan
Bernike
First Cataract
Dunqul Oasis
Nile River
Nile
Nabta Playa
Abu Simbel
Wadi Allaqi
Buhen
KUSH
Wadi Gabgaba

For many months each year, the Nile River flooded the nearby land. This helped turn desert into farmland. Early Egyptians used the rich soil along the Nile's riverbanks to grow food and raise animals.

LEARN MORE

When the Nile flooded it could cause great ruin too.

Upper and Lower

Over time, villages throughout Egypt began coming together. Then, the Egyptian civilization grew into two **kingdoms**. Lower Egypt was at the mouth of the Nile River in the north. Upper Egypt was in the drier valley to the south.

LEARN MORE

The water of the Nile River flows from north to south. That's why the more southern part of Egypt was called the Upper Kingdom.

Nile River today

One Kingdom

In about 3100 BCE, a king named Menes united, or brought together, the kingdoms of Upper and Lower Egypt. Menes, sometimes also called Narmer or Aha, became Egypt's first pharaoh, or king. He built new cities, such as the capital city of Memphis.

LEARN MORE

The kings of Upper Egypt wore a white crown. The kings of Lower Egypt wore a red crown. Rulers of the united lands sometimes wore a double crown that was both red and white.

Menes uniting Egypt

Egyptian god Horus in double crown

Around this time, ancient Egyptians began to use a form of writing called hieroglyphics. Hieroglyphics used pictures or **symbols** to stand for words and sounds. Much of what historians know about ancient Egypt comes from hieroglyphics painted on walls or **carved** into stone.

Rosetta Stone

LEARN MORE

The Rosetta Stone is a large piece of stone that has Greek, hieroglyphics, and another kind of writing on it called demotic. It is the reason we know how to read hieroglyphics!

hieroglyphics

Old Kingdom

Much of the history of ancient Egypt can be broken into three parts called kingdoms. The first part is the Old Kingdom, and it lasted from 2575 BCE until 2130 BCE. During the Old Kingdom, the Egyptians built the pyramids!

LEARN MORE

Ancient Egyptians built the pyramids to house the **tombs** of the pharaohs. Pyramids have a square base and four sides shaped like triangles. The sides meet at the top in a point.

Great Pyramids of Giza

Many Gods

In ancient Egypt, people believed in many gods. They thought these gods created, or made, and controlled their world. Pharaohs led the government as well as **religion** in Egypt. They were seen as a bridge between the gods and people.

Learn More

The main Egyptian god of the sun was Ra, or Re.

the sun god Ra

Middle Kingdom

The Middle Kingdom lasted from 1938 BCE until 1630 BCE. This was a time of growth. Pharaohs spread their power into nearby lands. It's likely the Egyptians traded with the Greek island of Crete and parts of Asia.

LEARN MORE

Some of the best art of ancient Egypt was made during the time of the Middle Kingdom.

Egyptian pharaoh,
Middle Kingdom

Takeover!

Invaders took over Egypt around 1630 BCE. The Hyksos from Asia ruled in the north. A group from other parts of Africa, the Kush, ruled in the south. About 90 years later, the Egyptians pushed them out. The New Kingdom, which followed, lasted from about 1540 BCE until 1075 BCE.

LEARN MORE

Not all pharaohs were men. Queen Hatshepsut ruled as pharaoh during the New Kingdom.

Queen Hatshepsut

New Kingdom

Ancient Egypt grew during the New Kingdom. Egyptian soldiers, or fighters, successfully pushed into Syria, among other lands around the Mediterranean Sea. Pharaohs built giant **statues** and buildings. One pharaoh, Ramses II, even built his own city called Per-Ramessu.

Learn More

One pharaoh of the New Kingdom, Tutankhamun—or Tut—became pharaoh at just 9 years old! Tut's tomb was discovered in 1922. His **mummy** was in it!

inside King Tut's tomb

An Empire Conquers

The rulers of Egypt's New Kingdom had to keep fighting off invaders. Egypt lost its strength and land it had **conquered** during the New Kingdom. Darius I of the Persian, or Achaemenid, **Empire** took over Egypt in 525 BCE.

Learn More

At its largest, the Persian Empire held the lands of present-day Turkey, Iran, and Egypt as well as parts of Afghanistan and Pakistan.

Darius I

A Great Ruler

Alexander the Great conquered the Persian-controlled Egypt in 332 BCE. It became part of his huge empire. The city of Alexandria was built during his rule. It became the new capital of Egypt. Alexandria was home to the Library of Alexandria, a center of great learning.

LEARN MORE

Alexander's general Ptolemy ruled Egypt after Alexander died. He became king and began a 300-year **dynasty**!

The Last Pharoah

The Roman Empire conquered Egypt around 30 BCE. It took power from the last pharaoh of Egypt, Cleopatra VII. Egypt remained part of the Roman Empire until about 395 CE when the empire broke in two.

Learn More

Cleopatra was part of Ptolemy's dynasty. She is known for working with Roman ruler Julius Caeser to stay in power in Egypt.

Timeline of Ancient Egypt

3100 BCE	Menes unites Upper Egypt and Lower Egypt into one kingdom.
2575–2130 BCE	Rulers during the Old Kingdom build the pyramids.
1938–1630 BCE	Egypt grows during the Middle Kingdom.
1540–1075 BCE	Rulers of the New Kingdom build statues and buildings.
525 BCE	The Persian Empire conquers Egypt.
332 BCE	Alexander the Great conquers Egypt and founds the city of Alexandria.
30 BCE	Egypt falls to the Roman Empire.

GLOSSARY

dynasty: Rulers that are part of the same family that rule for a long time.

carve: To cut into stone.

civilization: Organized society with written records and laws.

conquer: To take by force.

empire: A large area of land under the control of a single ruler.

invader: Someone who enters a place to take it over.

kingdom: A country ruled by a king or queen.

mummy: The dead body of a person that has been made ready for burial by being treated with oils and wrapped in strips of cloth.

religion: A belief in and way of honoring a god or gods.

statue: A figure, usually of a person or animal, that is made from stone or metal.

symbol: A picture, shape, or object that stands for something else.

tomb: A burial room.

FOR MORE INFORMATION

BOOKS

Hansen, Grace. *Daily Life.* Minneapolis, MN: Abdo Kids Jumbo, 2023.

Mather, Charis. *The Peculiar Past in Ancient Egypt.* Minneapolis, MN: Bearport Publishing Company, 2024.

WEBSITE

10 Facts About Ancient Egypt
www.natgeokids.com/uk/discover/history/egypt/ten-facts-about-ancient-egypt
Find out about ancient Egypt and what Egypt is like today.

Publisher's note to educators and parents: Our editors have carefully reviewed this website to ensure it is suitable for students. Many websites change frequently, however, and we cannot guarantee that a site's future contents will continue to meet our high standards of quality and educational value. Be advised that students should be closely supervised whenever they access the internet.

INDEX